Top 30 Most

Burger Recipes

A Burger Cookbook with Lamb, Chicken and Turkey

by Graham Bourdain

Disclaimer

Reasonable care has been taken to ensure that the information presented in this book is accurate. However, the reader should understand that the information provided does not constitute legal, medical or professional advice of any kind.

No Liability: this product is supplied "as is" and without warranties. All warranties, express or implied, are hereby disclaimed. Use of this product constitutes acceptance of the "No Liability" policy. If you do not agree with this policy, you are not permitted to use or distribute this product.

We shall not be liable for any losses or damages whatsoever

(including, without limitation, consequential loss or damage) directly or indirectly arising from the use of this product.

Table of Contents

Lamb Burgers

Chicken Burgers

Turkey Burgers

1. Goat Cheese Stuffed Lamb Burgers

Prep: 25 min. Cook: 15 min. Ready in: 40 min. Servings: 6

Ingredients:

1 tsp. olive oil

½ cup diced onion

2 pounds ground lamb

1 egg

1 cup bread crumbs

1 clove of minced garlic

3 tsp. salt

1 tbsp. ground black pepper

4 oz. soft goat cheese

1 tbsp. extra-virgin olive oil

1 tbsp. chopped fresh basil leaves

1 tbsp. chopped fresh oregano

6 burger buns

Cooking Directions:

Start by heating 1 tbsp. of olive in a pan over medium heat. Cook and stir the onions in the oil until they are soft and translucent, approx. 5 min.

Mix together the onions, lamb, egg, bread crumbs, garlic, salt and pepper.

Divide the mix into 6 even parts and roll them into balls.

Cover and refrigerate until ready to use.

Mix together the goat cheese, extra-virgin olive oil, basil, and oregano until well combined.

Cover and let the mix chill for 5 min.

Next up, preheat an outdoor grill for medium to high heat.

Take the meatballs and make an indentation in the center of the ball and fill up the indentation with a tablespoon of the goat cheese mix.

Evenly pull and form the meat patty around the goat cheese mix and in the process, make a burger shaped patty.

Repeat this process with the rest of the meatballs.

Grill the meat patties on the grill for approx. 8 min. per side or until they are no longer pink in the center.

Assemble the burgers and serve.

Enjoy

2. Mediterranean Lamb Burgers

Prep: 35 min. Cook: 10 min. Ready in: 45 min. Servings: 4

Ingredients:

1 pound ground lamb

½ pound ground beef

3 tsp. chopped fresh mint

1 tsp. minced fresh ginger root

1 tsp. minced garlic

1 tsp. salt

½ tsp. ground black pepper

16 oz. (1 container) Greek Yoghurt

½ zested lemon

1 clove minced garlic

½ tsp. salt

1 large sweet onion cut into ½ inch slices

4 slices green tomato

4 ciabatta sandwich rolls, sliced

8 oz. (1 package) sliced feta cheese

8 baby arugula leaves

Cooking Directions:

Start by preheating an outdoor grill on medium to high heat. Oil the grate lightly.

Mix the ground lamb, ground beef, mint, ginger, 1 tsp. garlic, 1 tsp salt and pepper in a large bowl.

Divide the mix into 4 evenly large portions and shape them in to patties.

Next, mix the Greek yoghurt, lemon zest, 1 clove garlic and ½ tsp. salt in a bowl. Cover the mix and refrigerate it for later.

Grill the patties on the preheated grill until the patties are grilled to your taste. Approx. 2 min. for medium-well and 3-4 min per side for well-done patties.

When the patties are about done add the slices of onion and green tomato to the grill and grill until lightly charred, approx. 1 min. on each side.

Now take the sliced ciabatta rolls and spread yoghurt sauce over them. Assemble each burger by placing the patty on the roll, and divide the feta cheese slices over the patties. Top it off with a slice of grilled tomato, grilled onion and 2 leaves of arugula and finish off with the top half of the roll and serve.

Enjoy

3. Maple Glazed Chipotle Goat Cheese Lamb Burgers

Prep: 40 min. Cook: 1 h 5 min. Ready in: 2 h 15 min. Servings: 4

Ingredients:

1 pound ground lamb

1 head garlic

6 oz. soft goat cheese

4 tbsp. minced chipotle peppers in adobo sauce

2 sprigs chopped fresh rosemary

2 tbsp. maple syrup

1 ½ tsp. salt

½ tsp. cracked black pepper

1 tsp. olive oil

2 tbsp. maple syrup

4 ciabatta buns, sliced

Cooking Directions:

Start by preheating the oven 300 degrees F (150 degrees C). Take the head of garlic and cut off the top of the head. Place the garlic onto an oven safe dish.

Bake the garlic until the cloves are golden brown and soft, approx. 1 hour. Remove the garlic from the oven and let it cool. Once the garlic has cooled enough to handle, squeeze it in a mixing bowl. Add the lamb, goat cheese, chipotle peppers, rosemary, 2 tbsp. maple syrup, salt and pepper. Mix it well. Take the mixture and form it into 4 evenly sized patties.

Heat the olive oil in a frying pan over medium-high heat. Sear the patties for approx. 1 min. on each. Reduce the heat to medium-low and continue cooking the patties to your liking, approx. 2 min. per side for medium-well.

Approx. 1 min. before the patties are ready, pour in the remaining 2 tbsp. of maple syrup. Allow the syrup to thicken and glaze the patties. Serve on toasted ciabatta buns.

Enjoy

4. Prosciutto Lamb Burgers

Prep: 20 min. Cook: 16 min. Ready in: 36 min. Servings: 4

Ingredients:

½ cup dried bread crumbs

¼ cup chopped fresh flat-leaf Italian parsley

1 large egg, lightly beaten

2 tbsp. whole milk

½ cup grated Pecorino Romano

¼ cup chopped sun-dried tomatoes

¾ tsp. salt

¾ tsp. freshly ground black pepper

1 pound ground lamb

6 large slices prosciutto, sliced medium thin.

¼ cup olive oil

Fresh basil leaves for topping

Fresh tomato slices for topping

Extra-virgin olive oil for drizzling

Balsamic vinegar for drizzling

6 burger buns

Cooking Directions:

Start by taking a large mixing bowl and combine the bread crumbs, parsley, egg, milk, cheese, sun-dried tomatoes, salt, and pepper.

Add the lamb and mix well. Divide the mixture into 6 evenly sized patties. Place the slices of prosciutto on a cutting board or some parchment paper. Take 1 of the patties and place it in the center of each slice of prosciutto and wrap the prosciutto around the burger.

Place a large frying pan over medium heat. Add the olive oil and heat for 2 min. Place the lamb patties, prosciutto-covered side down in the pan and cook over medium heat until the prosciutto is golden, approx. 6-8 min. Flip the patties and continue for approx. 6-8 min.

Remove the patties from the pan and start assembling the burgers.

Top each burger with 2-3 basil leaves, 1-2 slices of tomato and a drizzle of extra virgin- olive oil and balsamic vinegar and serve.

Enjoy

5. Pickled Feta Lamb Burgers

Prep: 2 h 15 min. Cook: 20 min. Ready in: 2 h 35 min. Servings: 4

Ingredients:

Patties:
Extra-virgin olive oil
2 red onions, 1 cut into ¼-inch dice and 1 sliced for garnish
Kosher salt
Pinch crushed red pepper
2 cloves garlic, finely smashed
1 ½ pounds ground lamb
½ bunch fresh dill, finely chopped
½ bunch fresh mint, finely chopped
2 sprigs fresh oregano, finely chopped
Zest of ½ lemon
4 burger buns
1 beef steak tomato, sliced for garnish
2 cups baby spinach, for garnish
Pickled Feta Spread:
1 cup champagne vinegar
1 tbsp. sugar
½ tbsp. kosher salt
2 mint tea bags
1 bay leaf
3 fresh mint stems
3 fresh dill stems
3 fresh oregano stems
8 oz. feta, coarsely crumbled
½ cup plain Greek Yoghurt

Cooking Directions:

Start by adding the vinegar, sugar, salt, tea bags, bay leaf and herbs stem to a small sauce pan along with 1 cup of water.

Heat the mix until the sugar and salt has dissolved. Remove from heat and let cool.

Place the feta in a small container. Add the vinegar mixture and make sure that the feta is submerged in the liquid. Let sit for a couple of hours outside the refrigerator.

Strain the feta from the pickling liquid and discard the tea bags, bay leaf and stems. Place the feta in a food processor and add the yoghurt. Pulse until fully combined.

Next coat a large frying pan with olive oil, add the diced onions and with salt and crushed red pepper.

Bring the pan to medium-high heat and cook the onion for approx. 3-4 min. Add the garlic and cook for another 2-4 min. Turn the heat off and let cool.

After this take, a large bowl and mix the lamb, the cooled onion mixture, the dill, mint, oregano, lemon zest and ½ to ¾ cups of water. Sprinkle with salt and mix well.

Preheat the frying again once more and divide the lamb mixture into 4 equal patties and sprinkle with salt. Cook the burgers for approx. 4-5 min. per side for medium-rare. When done, remove the patties from the pan and let them rest for 3-4 min.

Then take the burger buns and spread a layer of the pickled feta spread on both sides, add a patty and various garnish of your liking and serve.

Enjoy

6. Latin-Spiced Lamb Burgers

Prep: 30 min. Cook: 15 min. Ready in: 45 min. Servings: 6

Ingredients:

Patties:
1 ½ tsp. whole black pepper
½ tsp. coriander seeds
½ tsp. cumin seeds
¼ to ½ tsp. cayenne powder
2 cloves minced fresh garlic
Salt
2 pounds ground lamb
Sauce:
1/3 cup dried ancho chiles, caps removed and seeded
1/3 cup dried pulla, caps removed and seeded
1/3 cup dried pasilla, caps removed and seeded
1 cup water
1 tbsp. sour cream
¼ cup extra-virgin olive oil
1 small clove garlic, chopped
2 to 3 tbsp. fresh lime juice
½ tbsp. salt
Cream
Burgers:
6 burger buns
3 oz. Cotija cheese – Red onion, sliced – Tomato, sliced – Lettuce

Cooking Directions:

Start by adding pepper, coriander and cumin seeds to a dry pan and toast them until they start to crackle. Pour them straight into a coffee grinder and blend the seeds to a fine powder.

Then take a mixing bowl and add all the spices, garlic and salt to the lamb and mix it well. Form the mix into 6 evenly sized patties.

Moving on to the sauce. After weighing, open up the dried peppers to shake out the seeds. Put the peppers in a saucepan with the water and boil over medium heat until ¼ cup of liquid remains. Add the peppers, cooking liquid, sour cream, oil, garlic and lime to the blender, and blend it until smooth. Add salt and cream and blend again until the mix gets a saucy consistency.

Cook the lamb patties on a frying pan for approx. 4-5 min. per side for medium rare. Put about 1 tsp. of sauce on each side of the hamburger bun and crumble Cojita cheese on top. Assemble the burger with tomato slices, onion and lettuce and serve.

Enjoy

7. Garlic Yoghurt Lamb Burgers

Prep: 25 min. Cook: 10 min. Ready in: 35 min. Servings: 4

Ingredients:

1 ½ pounds ground lamb

1 medium yellow onion, peeled

1 tsp. allspice

1 ½ tsp. ground cumin

½ tsp. ground cinnamon

1 small red chile pepper, seeded and minced

1 egg, lightly beaten

A handful plain bread crumbs

Salt and freshly ground black pepper

1 tbsp. extra-virgin olive oil

1 cup Greek yoghurt

1 large clove garlic, peeled

¼ cup mint leaves, minced

½ red onion, peeled and sliced

½ small red cabbage, shredded

4 burger buns

Cooking Directions:

Start by putting the lamb in a mixing bowl. Using a box grater, grate the onion over the bowl, so the pulp and juices falls into the bowl. Add the spices, chile pepper, egg, bread crumbs, salt and pepper, to taste, and mix well.

Take the meat mixture and divide into 4 evenly sized patties.

Next, take a large frying pan and heat it over medium-high heat and coat it with oil. Cook the patties for approx. 4-5 min. on each side for medium rare.

While the patties cook, add yoghurt to a small bowl and grate the garlic into the yoghurt using a fine grater or zester. Add the mint and stir to combine.

Assemble the burgers with topping the patties with the yoghurt, sliced red onion and some shredded cabbage and serve.

Enjoy

8. Pickled Cucumber Relish and Five Spice Aioli Lamb Burgers

Prep: 1 h 20 min. Cook: 20 min. Ready in: 1 h 40 min. Servings: 4

Ingredients:

½ cup mayonnaise
juice of 1 lime
2 tsp. five-spice powder
1 tsp. coriander seeds
1 tsp. vegetable oil
½ red onion, small diced
1 red finger chile, seeded and diced
¼ cup white wine vinegar
¼ cup sugar
1 English cucumber, seeded and diced
Kosher salt
½ bunch fresh mint, stemmed and coarsely chopped
2 pounds ground lamb
1 shallot, minced
½ tbsp. fresh finger, minced
1 clove, minced
1 egg yolk
1 tbsp. five spice powder
Kosher salt and freshly ground black pepper
1 ripe tomato
4 burger buns

Cooking Directions:

Aioli

Start by taking a small bowl and mix together the mayonnaise, lime juice, and five-spice powder. Refrigerate the aioli until ready to use.

Relish

Next, take a sauté pan and bring it over medium-high heat, toast the coriander seeds until fragrant. Drizzle in the vegetable oil, add the red onion and cook until translucent. Stir frequently. Stir in the chile and white wine vinegar, and then sprinkle over the sugar, stirring until it is dissolved.

Add the cucumber to the pan, and cook for 5-7 min over medium heat, and reduce slightly until a light glaze consistency is achieved. Season the relish with salt, and let the mixture cool.

Just before serving the relish, stir in the mint, and season with salt, to taste.

Patties

Put the ground lamb, shallot, fresh ginger, garlic, egg yolk, and five-spice powder in a bowl, mix well. Season the mixture with salt and black pepper, to taste.

Divide and shape the meat mixture into 4 evenly sized patties. Place the patties in the refrigerator for 1 hour, to allow the flavors to infuse. Take a frying pan and heat it to medium-high heat and lightly oil it. Cook the lamb patties for approx. 4-5 min on each side for medium-rare.

Assemble the lamb patties together with toasted buns, slathered with the Five-Spice Aioli, Pickled Cucumber Relish, and sliced tomato and serve.

Enjoy

9. Lamb Moussaka Burger

Prep: 40 min. Cook: 25 min. Ready in: 1 h 20 min. Servings: 4

Ingredients:

2 tbsp. olive oil
1 yellow onion, diced
1 tsp. salt
2 cups diced eggplant
3 cloves garlic, crushed
1 tsp. freshly ground black pepper
½ tsp. cumin
¼ tsp. ground cinnamon
¼ tsp. dried oregano
2 tsp. tomato paste
1 ½ tbsp. olive oil
2 tbsp. flour
1 cup cold milk
1 pinch ground nutmeg
1 pinch cayenne pepper
1 pinch freshly ground black pepper
½ cup grated Parmesan cheese
1 pound ground lamb
salt to taste
8 slices tomato
1 tbsp. chopped fresh mint
1 tbsp. rice vinegar
1 tbsp. olive oil
4 burger buns

Cooking Directions:

Start by heating 2 tbsp. olive oil in a skillet over medium-high heat. Cook and stir diced onion with 1 tsp. salt until onion is slightly translucent, approx. 5 min. Add the eggplant, reduce the heat to medium, and cook and stir until the eggplant is softened, approx. 3-5 min.

Stir garlic, 1 tsp. black pepper, cumin, cinnamon, and oregano into the eggplant mixture. Cook and stir until fragrant, approx. 1 min. Add tomato paste, cook until heated, approx. 2 min. Transfer the mix to a plate and let it cool completely. Cover the plate with plastic wrap and refrigerate until completely chilled.

Whisk 1 ½ tbsp. olive oil and flour together in a saucepan over medium-high heat until golden and bubbling, approx. 2-3 min. Pour milk into the mix, whisking constantly while it forms into a smooth, thick sauce, approx. 3-5 min. Season with nutmeg, a pinch black pepper, and a pinch cayenne pepper. Remove from heat and stir Parmesan cheese into the milk mixture until it is melted.

Put tomato slices in a bowl. Season tomatoes with chopped mint, a pinch of salt, and a pinch of black pepper. Pour rice vinegar over the top and gently turn the tomato slices in the bowl until covered.

Combine lamb, chilled eggplant mix and a pinch of salt together in a bowl. Divide the meat mix into 4 evenly sized patties.

Heat 1 tbsp. olive oil in a frying pan over medium-high heat. Cook the patties on each side until medium-rare, approx. 4 min.

Spread cheese sauce on both sides of each toasted hamburger bun. Assemble the burger with tomato slices atop the burger and serve.

Enjoy

10. Lamb Burgers with Green Raita Sauce and Red Onions

Prep: 25 min. Cook: 6 min. Ready in: 31 min. Servings: 8

Ingredients:

Green Raita Sauce
1 cup plain Greek yoghurt
A handful cilantro leaves
A handful mint leaves
1 clove garlic, peeled and grated or mashed into paste
Pinch salt
1 lime, juiced
Sliders
4 slices red onion
1 lime, juiced
Extra-virgin olive oil, for drizzling
Salt and freshly ground black pepper
2 pounds ground lamb
2 large cloves garlic, grated or finely chopped
1 red or green chile, fincly chopped
1-inch piece ginger, grated or minced
1 tsp. turmeric, ground cumin, ground coriander or onion powder
Pinch ground cinnamon
Baby spinach leaves
8 slider rolls

Cooking Directions:

Start by putting all the ingredients for the sauce in a food processor and process until smooth.

Put the red onion rings in a bowl and separate the rings. Add the lime juice and drizzle with extra-virgin olive oil. Season with salt and pepper, to taste.

Add the lamb to a mixing bowl along with the garlic, chile, ginger, spices, cinnamon, and salt and pepper, to taste. Mix well.

Divide the meat mix into 8 evenly slider sized patties.

Next, take a large skillet and heat it up with a drizzle of extra-virgin olive oil over medium-high heat.

Add the patties and cook them until medium-rare, approx. 4-5 min. per side.

Assemble the burger by putting a few leaves of spinach on each of the bun bottoms and add the patty. Top with onions and green sauce to taste. Cover with top bun and serve.

Enjoy

11. Chicken Burgers with Garlic-Rosemary Mayonnaise

Prep: 20 min. Cook: 15 min. Ready in: 35 min. Servings: 4

Ingredients:

Mayonnaise

1 cup mayonnaise

¼ cup chopped fresh rosemary leaves

1 clove garlic, minced

Patties

1 pound ground chicken

½ teaspoon kosher salt

¼ teaspoon freshly ground black pepper

¼ cup olive oil

1 cup arugula, divided

4 burger buns

Cooking Directions:

Start by taking a small bowl and mix together the mayonnaise, garlic and rosemary. Set aside when done.

Next, take a grill pan and place it over medium-high heat. Take a large mixing bowl and add the ground chicken, ½ tsp. salt, ¼ tsp. pepper, and ½ of the mayonnaise mixture. Gently combine the ingredients and form the meat mixture into 4 evenly sized patties. Place the burgers on the pan and cook for approx. 6 min. on each side.

After cooking transfer the patties to paper towels and let them rest for a few minutes.

Brush each side of the burger buns with olive oil and 1 tsp. of the mayonnaise mixture. Put them on the pan for approx. 1-2 min. until slightly golden.

Assemble the burgers by spreading the remaining mayonnaise mixture on the toasted buns. Place the chicken patties on the buns and top each one off with ¼ cup of arugula. Finish with the top half of the bun and serve.

Enjoy

12. Aloha Chicken Burgers

Prep: 20 min. Cook: 30 min. Ready in: 1 h 20 min. Servings: 2

Ingredients:

2 skinless, boneless chicken breast halves

¼ cup soy sauce

3 slices thick cut bacon

2 hamburger buns

1 tbsp. softened butter

¼ teriyaki sauce

2 slices Swiss cheese

2 tbsp. mayonnaise

2 slices pineapple

2 slices tomato

2 slices of iceberg lettuce

Cooking Directions:

Start by placing the chicken breasts into a plastic zipper bag with soy sauce, seal the bag, and let them marinate in the refrigerator for 30 min. While the chicken is marinating, place the bacon in a large skillet, and cook over medium-high heat until evenly browned, approx. 10 min. Drain the bacon slices on paper towels and set aside.

Take the burger buns and spread butter onto them.

Turn on the oven and heat it up to 400 degrees F (200 degrees C)

Remove the chicken from the soy sauce, discard the excess sauce. Loosely roll up the marinated chicken breast with teriyaki sauce in foil, and bake in the oven for approx. 20 min. Once the chicken is done, open the foil and place a slice of Swiss cheese on each chicken breast to melt it.

Lightly warm the burger buns in the oven.

Assemble the burgers by spreading the sides of each bun with mayonnaise. Top each bottom bun with a cooked chicken breast, 1 ½ slices of bacon, a slice of pineapple, a slice from a head of lettuce, a slice of tomato, the top bun and serve.

Enjoy

13. Asian Chicken Burgers

Prep: 10 min. Cook: 20 min. Ready in: 30 min. Servings: 4

Ingredients:

Nonstick cooking spray

1 small carrot

1 small red onion, halved

¼ cup panko (Japanese breadcrumbs)

¼ cup hoisin sauce

1 tbsp. grated peeled ginger

4 tsp. low-sodium soy sauce

3 tsp. hot Asian chili sauce, such as sambal oelek

8 oz. white mushrooms, thinly sliced

2 tsp. toasted sesame oil

Juice of 1 lime

4 burger buns

Cooking Directions:

Start by preheating the oven to 375 degrees F (190 degrees C). Mist a baking sheet with cooking spray. Grate the carrot and ½ onion into a bowl. Add the chicken, panko, 2 tbsp. hoisin sauce, ginger, 3 tsp. soy sauce and 1 tsp. sambal oelek and mix well. Take the chicken mix and divide it into 4 evenly sized patties and place them on the prepared baking sheet. Bake until cooked through, approx. 20 min. While the patties are cooking, thinly slice the remaining ½ onion. Put the onions, mushrooms, sesame oil, lime juice and the remaining 1 tsp. soy sauce in a bowl. Mix the remaining 2 tsps. hoisin sauce and 2 tsp. sambal oelek with 1 tsp. water in another bowl. Warm the burger buns in the oven. Assemble the burgers by putting the patties on the bun with a drizzle of the hoisin-sambal sauce and some of the mushroom mixture and serve.

Enjoy

14. Cilantro Chicken Burgers with Avocado

Prep: 15 min. Cook: 10 min. Ready in: 25 min. Servings: 4

Ingredients:

1 pound ground chicken

½ cup chopped fresh cilantro

1 tbsp. soy sauce

1 tbsp. garlic powder

1 tsp. lime juice

1 tsp. ground ginger

1 tbsp. ground black pepper

cooking spray

4 burger buns

1 avocado, peeled, pitted, and sliced

¼ cup ranch dressing

Cooking Directions:

Start by mixing the ground chicken, cilantro, soy sauce, garlic powder, lime juice, ground ginger and ground black pepper together in a large bowl.

Take the chicken mix and divide it into 4 evenly sized patties.

Prepare a skillet with cooking spray and place it over medium heat.

Cook the patties in the skillet until medium-rare, approx. 4-5 min. per side.

Assemble the burgers by placing the patties on the buns with slices of avocado and 1 tbsp. ranch dressing.

Enjoy

15. BBQ Chicken Burgers with Slaw

Prep: 10 min. Cook: 20 min. Ready in: 30 min. Servings: 4

Ingredients:

1 tbsp. butter

1 small red onion, ½ finely chopped, ½ thinly sliced

2 cloves garlic, finely chopped

2 tbsp. tomato paste

1 tsp. sugar

1 tbsp. Worcestershire sauce

1 tbsp. hot sauce

1 ¼ pounds ground chicken

1 tbsp. grill seasoning

3 tbsp. extra-virgin olive oil, divided

2 tbsp. honey

1 lemon, juiced

3 rounded tbsp. sweet pickle relish

2 cups shredded cabbage mix

Salt and pepper

4 burger buns

Cooking Directions:

Start by heating a frying pan over medium heat, melt the butter. Add chopped onions, garlic and tomato paste and cook them for approx. 5 min. to soften and sweeten. Sprinkle in the sugar and remove from heat. Cool in a bowl for 5 min. Add tomato paste mixture, Worcestershire sauce, hot sauce to the bowl and mix well.

Add the ground chicken and grill seasoning to the bowl and form 4 evenly sized patties from the mix.

Take a frying pan and heat 1 tbsp. extra-virgin olive oil in a nonstick skillet over medium-high heat. Cook the patties approx. 6 min. on each side.

Combine the honey, lemon juice and remaining extra-virgin olive oil in a bowl. Add relish, cabbage mix, sliced onions and season with salt and pepper. Mix well.

Serve the patties on bun bottoms topped with slaw and bun tops.

Enjoy

16. Grilled Hawaiian Chicken and Pineapple Burgers

Prep: 15 min. Cook: 11 min. Ready in: 1 h 26 min. Servings: 6

Ingredients:

6 skinless, boneless chicken breast halves, pounded to ¼ inch thickness

1 cup Hawaiian style marinade

6 pineapple rings

6 slices provolone cheese

6 onion rolls, split

6 tbsp. thousand island salad dressing

6 leaves romaine lettuce

6 slices tomato

Cooking Directions:

Start by placing the chicken breast halves into a large resealable bag and pour in the marinade. Let the chicken marinate in the refrigerator for at least 1 hour or up to overnight.

Take a grill pan and heat it to medium-high heat. Lightly oil it. Remove the chicken from the marinade and discard the excess marinade.

Cook the chicken pieces on the pan for approx. 5 min. per side or until cooked through. 5 min. before they are done, place the pineapple rings on the pan and cook for a couple of min. per side. Place the pineapple slices on top of the pieces of chicken and top with a slice of cheese. Allow the cheese to melt for a minute or two.

Toast the buns, if desired.

Assemble the burgers by placing the chicken, pineapple and cheese onto the bottom buns. Top with lettuce and tomato. Spread the thousand island dressing onto the top buns and place onto the burgers.

Enjoy

17. Chicken Cordon Bleu Burgers

Prep: 10 min. Cook: 12 min. Ready in: 22 min. Servings: 4

Ingredients:

2 tsp. vegetable or olive oil, plus more for drizzling

4 slices Canadian bacon

2 pounds ground chicken breast

2 tsp. sweet paprika

2 tsp. poultry seasoning

2 tsp. grill seasoning

1 shallot, finely chopped

4 deli slices Swiss cheese

2/3 cup mayonnaise

3 tbsp. Dijon mustard

2 tbsp. freshly chopped tarragon leaves, 4 sprigs

4 burger buns

8 leaves leaf lettuce

1 ripe tomato, thinly sliced

Cooking Directions:

Start by preheating a grill pan to medium-high heat. Add 2 tbsp. of oil and Canadian bacon. Caramelize the bacons edges, approx. 1-2 min. on each side. Remove the bacon to a piece of foil and fold the foil over loosely to keep the bacon warm. Combine chicken, paprika, poultry seasoning, grill seasoning and shallot. Divide the chicken mix into 4 evenly sized patties. Drizzle the patties with oil place on the hot grill pan. Cook for approx. 5 min. on each side, until the chicken is cooked through.

Top the patties with reserved cooked Canadian bacon and Swiss cheese. Cover the pan loosely with tin foil. Turn of the pan and let the cheese melt, approx. 2 min.

Mix mayonnaise, mustard, tarragon.

Brush the buns with sauce and place the Cordon Bleu patties on the bun bottoms and top with lettuce and tomato. Top off with the bun tops and serve.

Enjoy

18. Chicken Cheddar and Guacamole Burgers

Prep: 15 min. Cook: 10 min. Ready in: 28 min. Servings: 4

Ingredients:

1 ½ pound ground chicken

½ cup minced yellow onion

1/3 cup minced fresh cilantro

1/3 cup shredded Cheddar cheese

2 cloves garlic, minced

1 jalapeno pepper, seeded and minced

½ lime, juiced

1 tsp. ground cumin

1 tsp. paprika

½ tsp. Kosher salt

½ tsp. ground black pepper

4 slices Cheddar cheese

4 burger buns

¼ cup guacamole

4 tsp. chopped fresh cilantro

Cooking Directions:

Start by taking a grill pan and heating it to medium-high heat. Lightly oil the pan.

Mix the ground chicken, 1/3 cup cilantro, Cheddar cheese, garlic, onion, jalapeno pepper, lime juice, cumin, paprika, salt, and pepper together in a bowl.

Take the chicken mix and divide it into 4 evenly sized patties.

Cook the patties on the grill pan for approx. 3-4 min. on each side. Once the patty is flipped the first time top it off with a slice of Cheddar cheese and let it melt for the duration.

Once the chicken patties are cooked throughout transfer them to a plate to rest until juices are reabsorbed into the meat, approx. 3 min.

Assemble the burgers by placing a chicken patty on the bottom bun, top off with guacamole and cilantro. Put top bun on and serve.

Enjoy

19. Coconut Basil Chicken Burgers with Thai Peanut Pesto

Prep: 45 min. Cook: 8 min. Ready in: 53 min. Servings: 6

Ingredients:

Asian Pear Slaw
1 tbsp. fresh lime juice
1 tsp. sugar
1 Asian pear, peeled and cut into thin sticks
1 medium carrot, peeled and cut into thin sticks

Thai Peanut Pesto
1/2 cup roasted and salted peanuts
½ cup fresh basil leaves
¼ cup fresh cilantro leaves
2 tbsp. unsweetened shredded coconut
2 tbsp. roasted peanut oil
¼ tsp. sea salt
1/3 cup quartered cherry tomatoes

Patties
1 can unsweetened coconut milk
1 lime, zest grated
1 tbsp. fresh lime juice
1 tsp. Thai red curry paste
2 pounds coarsely ground chicken thighs
½ cup panko (Japanese bread crumbs)
2 tsp. sea salt
Vegetable oil
6 burger buns

Cooking Directions:

Start by preparing the Asian Pear Slaw. Whisk together the lime juice and sugar in a bowl to dissolve the sugar. Add the pear and carrot and mix well. Cover and chill until time to serve.

To prepare the Thai Peanut Pesto, place all of the ingredients except the tomatoes in a small food processor. Process briefly until the mixture forms a coarse paste. Transfer to a bowl and gently stir in the tomatoes. Cover and set aside.

To prepare the patties combine the coconut milk, lime zest, and lime juice in a sauce pan and bring it to a simmer. Continue cooking until the mixture is thickened and reduced to 2/3 cup, approx. 15 min. Add the curry paste to the mixture and whisk until smooth. Transfer to a bowl to cool.

Place the chicken in a mixing bowl. Add the cooled coconut milk mixture, basil, panko and salt. Mix the ingredients together gently, but thoroughly. Divide the mixture into 6 evenly sized patties and make a slight indentation in the center of each patty.

Take a grill pan and heat it to medium-high heat. Oil it lightly. Place the patties on the pan and cook on each side, approx. 4-5 min.

Toast the buns, if desired.

Assemble the burgers by putting slaw on the bottom buns. Top each one off with a patty, a dollop of the pesto, bun tops and serve.

Enjoy

20. Greek Chicken Burgers with Feta

Prep: 15 min. Cook: 10 min. Ready in: 25 min. Servings: 5

Ingredients:

1 pound ground chicken

½ cup dry bread crumbs

1 egg

1 tbsp. lemon juice

2 tbsp. chopped sun-dried tomatoes

1 tbsp. chopped fresh basil

3 tsp. chopped fresh oregano

salt and pepper to taste

2 oz. crumbled feta cheese

Cooking Directions:

Start by heating a grill pan over medium-high heat. Lightly oil the pan. Mix the chicken, bread crumbs, egg, lemon juice, sun-dried tomatoes, basil, oregano, salt, and pepper together in a bowl. Mix well. Divide the chicken mix into 5 evenly sized patties. Divide the feta cheese between the 5 patties and place a portion of the feta cheese atop each patty. Fold the chicken patties around the cheese, so that the cheese is in the center.

Cook the patties on the grill pan for approx. 5-6 min. per side.

Assemble the burgers with extra garnish of your own desire.

Enjoy

21. Turkey Burger with Caramelized Onions and Spicy Sweet Mayo

Prep: 15 min. Cook: 20 min. Ready in: 35 min. Servings: 5

Ingredients:

Spicy Sweet Mayo
1 cup light mayonnaise
¼ cup coarse-grain mustard
¼ cup honey
1 tbsp. prepared horseradish
Hot pepper sauce, to taste
1 tsp. ground cayenne pepper
Burgers
1 ¼ pound ground turkey breast
½ large onion, grated
1 jalapeno pepper, seeded and minced
2 tbsp. barbeque sauce
2 tbsp. Worcestershire sauce
¼ tsp. liquid smoke flavoring
1 tbsp. steak seasoning
1 tsp. dry mesquite flavored seasoning mix
1 tbsp. olive oil
½ large onion, sliced
5 burger buns

Cooking Directions:

Start by taking a bowl and mix together the mayonnaise, mustard, honey, horseradish, hot pepper sauce, and cayenne pepper. Cover it and cool in the refrigerator.

Mix ground turkey, grated onion, jalapeno, barbeque sauce, Worcestershire sauce, liquid smoke, steak seasoning, and mesquite seasoning in a large bowl. Divide the turkey mix into 5 evenly sized patties.

Next, take a frying pan and heat it over medium-high heat. Drizzle it with olive oil. Stir in the onion and cook until softened and translucent, approx. 5 min. Reduce the heat to medium-low, and continue cooking and stirring until the onion is very tender and dark brown, approx. 15-20 min. more.

Cook the patties in a frying pan over medium heat for approx. 6 min. per side.

Assemble the burgers by taking the bottom bun, place the patty and top off with spicy sweet mayo and caramelized onions. Place top bun and serve.

Enjoy

22. Jerk Turkey Burgers with Mango Slaw

Prep: 25 min. Cook: 10 min. Ready in: 35 min. Servings: 4

Ingredients:

1 pound ground turkey

1 tbsp. jerk seasoning, plus more for sprinkling

1 small green apple, peeled and grated

½ cup finely chopped scallions

¼ cup panko (Japanese breadcrumbs)

Kosher salt and freshly ground pepper

¼ cup mayonnaise, plus more for brushing

¼ cup mango chutney, roughly chopped

3 cups shredded green cabbage

1 carrot, shredded

Canola oil, for the grill pan

4 burger buns

Cooking Directions:

Start by taking a grill pan and heat it to medium-high heat. Mix the turkey jerk seasoning, apple, 1/4 cup scallions and the panko in a bowl. Season with salt and pepper.

Divide the mix into 4 evenly sized patties and put them aside and refrigerate.

Whisk the mayonnaise and chutney in a large bowl. Add the cabbage, carrot and the remaining 1/4 cup scallions, season with salt and pepper and toss to coat.

Drizzle the grill pan with canola oil. Cook the turkey patties until browned and cooked through, approx. 4-5 min per side.

Brush the cut sides of the bun with mayonnaise and sprinkle with jerk seasoning. Toast on the grill pan for about 30 sec.

Assemble the burgers by putting the patty on the bottom bun. Top off with slaw, top bun and serve.

Enjoy

23. Spicy Chipotle Turkey Burgers

Prep: 25 min. Cook: 10 min. Ready in: 35 min. Servings: 4

Ingredients:

1 pound ground turkey

½ cup finely chopped onion

2 tbsp. chopped fresh cilantro

1 chipotle chili in adobo sauce, finely chopped

1 tsp. garlic powder

1 tsp. onion powder

1 tsp. seasoned salt

¼ tsp. black pepper

4 slices mozzarella cheese

4 burger buns

Cooking Directions:

Start by heating a grill pan over medium-high heat. Lightly oil it.

Take a mixing bowl and add the turkey, onion, chipotle chile pepper, garlic powder, onion powder, seasoned salt, and black pepper.

Divide the turkey mix into 4 evenly sized patties.

Cook the patties on the grill pan for approx. 4 min per side. Place the mozzarella slices on the patties 2 min. before they are ready.

Assemble the burgers with garnish of your desire and serve.

Enjoy

24. Southwest Turkey Burgers

Prep: 10 min. Cook: 15 min. Ready in: 25 min. Servings: 4

Ingredients:

8 slices turkey bacon

1 1/3 pounds ground turkey breast

2 cloves garlic, finely chopped

1 large shallot, finely chopped

2 tbsp. chopped fresh thyme leaves *or* 1 tsp. dried thyme leaves

2 tbsp. chopped fresh cilantro leaves

½ small bell pepper, seeded and finely chopped

1 serrano or jalapeno pepper, seeded and finely chopped

2 tsp. ground cumin

1-2 tsp. cayenne hot sauce

2 tsp. grill seasoning blend

Vegetable oil or olive oil, for drizzling

½ pound deli sliced pepper jack cheese

1 cup sweet red pepper relish

Red leaf lettuce

4 burger buns

Cooking Directions:

Start by chopping the garlic and the vegetables.

Take a frying pan and cook the bacon over medium-high heat until crisp. Discard the excess grease from the pan and return it to heat.

While the bacons cooks, take a bowl and mix the ground turkey, garlic, shallot, thyme, cilantro, bell pepper, serrano or jalapeno pepper, cumin, hot pepper sauce and grill seasoning.

Divide the mixture into 4 evenly sized patties and drizzle them with vegetable oil.

Cook the patties on the frying pan at medium-high heat for approx. 5-6 min. on each side. Place sliced cheese over the patties in the last 2 min. of cooking and let it melt.

Assemble the patties in the buns and top with 2 slices of cooked, crisp bacon, sweet relish and red leaf lettuce. Put on the top bun and serve.

Enjoy

25. Black Bean Turkey Burgers with Salsa and Avocado

Prep: 20 min. Cook: 15 min. Ready in: 35 min. Servings: 4

Ingredients:

Salsa
4 large ripe tomatoes, diced
1 small onion, finely chopped
1 jalapeno pepper, seeded, deveined, and chopped
3 tbsp. chopped fresh cilantro
1 tbsp. olive oil
2 tbsp. lime juice
½ can black beans, rinsed, drained, and lightly mashed
1 cup frozen corn kernels, thawed
Patties
¼ cup olive oil
1 ¼ pounds ground turkey
½ can black beans, rinsed, drained, and lightly mashed
1 cup crushed tortilla chips
Pinch of salt
Pinch of pepper
Pinch of garlic powder
Pinch of onion powder
1 tbsp. chile powder
1 tbsp. ground cumin
1 avocado, halved, peeled, pitted, and firmly diced
Sour cream

Cooking Directions:

Start by taking a large bowl, take all of the ingredients for the salsa and combine and stir them together. Cover the bowl and chill the salsa until ready for use.

Next, take a frying pan and place it over medium-high heat. In a bowl, combine the turkey, beans, tortilla chips, salt, pepper, garlic powder, onion powder, chile powder and cumin. Mix well.

Divide the turkey mix into 4 evenly sized patties.

Cook the patties until they are cooked through, approx. 5-6 min per side. Transfer the patties to a paper towel-lined plate to drain.

Assemble the burgers by placing the patties on the bottom buns. Spoon salsa mixture on top and finally avocado slices and sour cream. Finish with the top bun and serve.

Enjoy

26. Asian Turkey Burgers

Prep: 25 min. Cook: 8 min. Ready in: 1 h 33 min. Servings: 6

Ingredients:

¼ cup bulgur wheat

½ cup boiling water

¼ cup rice wine vinegar

1 tsp. sugar

Kosher salt and freshly ground black pepper

¼ seedless cucumber, sliced 1/8-inch thick

¼ small red onion, thinly sliced

¼ cup plain low-fat yoghurt

1 tsp. chile garlic sauce

12 oz. lean ground turkey

2 tbsp. hoisin sauce

2 scallions, chopped

1 tsp. grated ginger

1 clove garlic, grated

2 tbsp. chopped cilantro, plus ¼ cup whole leaves

2 tsp. vegetable oil

4 burger buns

Cooking Directions:

Start by taking a bowl, add the bulgur and the boiling water. Cover with plastic wrap and set aside until the bulgur is tender, approx. 45 min. to 1 hour.

Meanwhile, take a bowl and whisk the vinegar and sugar with a generous seasoning of salt and pepper until dissolved. Add the cucumber and onion mix well and set aside to marinate for approx. 30 min.

In a separate bowl mix the yoghurt and chile garlic sauce. Season with salt and pepper and set aside.

Drain the bulgur and add the turkey, hoisin, scallions, ginger, garlic and chopped cilantro and mix until just combined.

Divide the turkey mix into 4 evenly sized patties.

Take a frying pan and put it over medium heat until very hot. Lightly drizzle both sides of each patty with oil and place on the frying pan. Cook the patties until they are cooked through, approx. 3-4 min per side.

Drain the pickled vegetables and mix with the whole cilantro leaves.

Assemble the burgers by spreading some spicy yoghurt sauce on the top and bottom of each bun and top with a patty and some pickles.

Enjoy

27. Apple Maple Turkey Burgers with Maple-Dijon Sauce

Prep: 10 min. Cook: 15 min. Ready in: 25 min. Servings: 4

Ingredients:

Maple-Dijon Sauce

¼ cup mayonnaise

1 tbsp. Dijon mustard

2 tbsp. real maple syrup

Patties

1 ¼ pounds ground turkey breast

¼ cup real bacon bits

½ cup chunky applesauce

1 tsp. poultry seasoning

2 tbsp. real maple syrup

½ tsp. salt

¼ tsp. ground black pepper

4 burger buns

Cooking Directions:

Start by taking a grill pan and place it over medium heat. Lightly oil it, when ready to start cooking.

To prepare the Maple-Dijon Sauce take a bowl, add the mayonnaise, Dijon mustard, 2 tbsp. maple syrup, stir and mix well. When mixed, set aside.

To prepare the patties take a bowl and mix together the turkey, bacon bits, chunky applesauce, poultry seasoning, maple syrup, salt and pepper. Divide the turkey mix into 4 evenly sized patties.

Cook the patties on the grill pan for approx. 5-6 min. per side.

Assemble the burgers by placing the patty on the bottom bun with traditional burger condiments and a dollop of maple-Dijon sauce. Finish with the top bun and serve.

Enjoy

28. Tex-Mex Turkey Burgers with Avocado Mayonnaise

Prep: 15 min. Cook: 8 min. Ready in: 23 min. Servings: 4

Ingredients:

1 ¼ pounds lean ground turkey

2 cloves garlic, grated

2 tsp. hot smoked paprika

Kosher salt and freshly ground pepper

1 avocado, halved

3 tbsp. mayonnaise

1 lime, juiced

1 tbsp. vegetable oil

4 slices pepper jack cheese

Shredded lettuce

4 burger buns

Cooking Directions:

Start by taking a bowl. Add the turkey, garlic, paprika, ¾ tsp. salt and a few grinds of pepper. Mix well.

Divide the turkey mix into 4 evenly sized patties, cover and set aside.

Combine ½ avocado, the mayonnaise, lime juice and ¼ tsp salt in a bowl, mash until smooth. Thinly slice the remaining ½ avocado and season with salt and pepper. Set aside for topping.

Next, take a frying pan and heat it over medium-high heat and drizzle it with vegetable oil. Add the patties and cook until browned, approx., 3-4 min per side. Place a slice of cheese on top of each patty, when there is about 1 min. remaining and let the cheese melt.

Meanwhile, toast the buns, spread the avocado mayonnaise on the cut sides.

Assemble the burgers by placing a patty on each bun. Top off with lettuce, the sliced avocados, condiments of your desire. Finish off with the bun top and serve.

Enjoy

29. Turkey Burgers with Prosciutto and Melon

Prep: 25 min. Cook: 20 min. Ready in: 45 min. Servings: 6

Ingredients:

2 pounds ground turkey

2 tbsp. grated onion

2 cloves minced garlic

4 tbsp. chopped basil leaves, divided

1 tsp. seasoned salt

½ tsp. black pepper

2 tbsp. olive oil

6 slices prosciutto

½ cup mayonnaise

2 tsp. lemon juice

6 slices smoked provolone

6 slices cantaloupe

Cooking Directions:

Start by taking a grill pan and put it over medium-high heat. Next, add the ground turkey, grated onion, garlic, 2 tbsp. basil, seasoned and salt and pepper. Mix well. Divide the turkey mix into 6 evenly sized patties. Set aside.

Drizzle the grill pan with olive oil and place the patties on the grill pan.

Cook the patties until cooked through, approx. 5-6 min. per side. While the patties are cooking, preheat a frying pan on medium-high heat. Place prosciutto slices on the pan and cook until crispy. Set aside.

When the patties are cooked, top with provolone and heat until melted. Transfer the patties from the grill pan to a plate. Cover with foil to keep them warm. Cut cantaloupe slices to fit the burger buns. Assemble the burgers by spreading mayonnaise on both cut sides of the bun. Place a patty on the bottom bun. Top the patties with slices of prosciutto and cantaloupe. Finish off with the top bun and serve.

Enjoy

30. Turkey Bacon Double Cheese Burgers with Fire Roasted Tomato Sauce

Prep: 15 min. Cook: 30 min. Ready In: 45 min. Servings: 4

Ingredients:

1 tbsp. Extra-virgin olive oil, plus extra for drizzling

8 slices turkey bacon

2 ½ pounds ground turkey breast

2 green onions, finely chopped

A handful cilantro, finely chopped

1 tbsp. chipotle chili powder

1 ½ tsp. smoked sweet paprika

Salt and freshly ground black pepper

2 tsp. zest and the juice of 2 limes

1 red onion, chopped

1 tbsp. Worcestershire sauce

2 tbsp. brown sugar

1 can fire-roasted diced tomatoes, lightly drained

2 rounded tbsp. grainy mustard

8 slices pepper jack cheese

4 burger buns

Cooking Directions:

Start by taking a frying pan and heating it over medium-high heat. Drizzle it lightly with olive oil and add the turkey bacon. Cook until crisp, approx. 3 min. on each side.

While the bacon cooks, combine the turkey breast, green onions, cilantro, chipotle, paprika, salt and pepper, lime zest and juice. Mix the turkey breast with seasonings and divide the turkey mix to 8 evenly sized patties.

Cook the first 4 patties in the pan for approx. 3-4 min on each side. Remove the patties from the pan and place onto a plate and loosely cover with foil to keep warm.

While the first batch of burgers cook heat 1 tbsp. oil in a sauce pot over medium-high heat. Add onions and soften 3-4 min, season with salt and pepper and then add Worcestershire sauce, brown sugar, tomatoes, and mustard.

Let the sauce cook on low.

Add the second batch of burger s to the frying pan and cook for approx. 3-4 min. on each side. Top with a slice of cheese and 2 pieces of bacon. Loosely cover the pan with foil to let the cheese melt, approx. 1 min.

Assemble the burgers by placing a patty on the bottom bun, add some fire roasted tomato sauce and then another patty. Finish it off with the top bun and serve.

Enjoy

Thank you for purchasing
Top 30 Most Delicious Burger Recipes.

We hope you found the recipes as tasteful and delicious as we do.

Please show your support and love for burgers by leaving a review on Amazon.

Make sure to check out all the other delicious recipes in the Top 30 Most Delicious cookbook series.

Printed in Great Britain
by Amazon

34999661R00037